WILLIAM

SHAKESPEARE

PLAYWRIGHT AND POET

SPECIAL LIVES IN HISTORY THAT BECOME

Signature LIVES

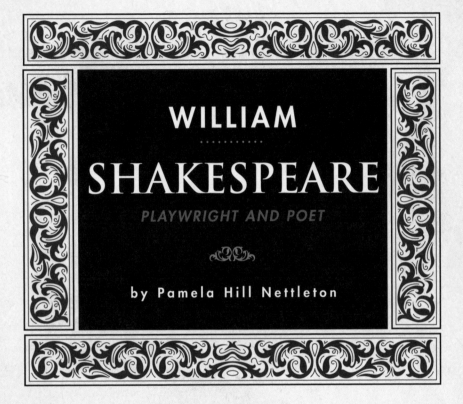

WILLIAM
SHAKESPEARE
PLAYWRIGHT AND POET

by Pamela Hill Nettleton

Content Adviser: Andrew Elfenbein, Ph.D.,
Professor, Department of English,
University of Minnesota

Reading Adviser: Rosemary G. Palmer, Ph.D.,
Department of Literacy, College of Education,
Boise State University

COMPASS POINT BOOKS ◆ MINNEAPOLIS, MINNESOTA

Compass Point Books
3109 West 50th Street, #115
Minneapolis, MN 55410

Visit Compass Point Books on the Internet at *www.compasspointbooks.com*
or e-mail your request to *custserv@compasspointbooks.com.*

Editor: Jennifer VanVoorst
Lead Designer: Jaime Martens
Photo Researcher: Svetlana Zhurkina
Page Production: Heather Griffin
Cartographer: XNR Productions, Inc.
Educational Consultant: Diane Smolinski

Managing Editor: Catherine Neitge
Art Director: Keith Griffin
Production Director: Keith McCormick
Creative Director: Terri Foley

Library of Congress Cataloging-in-Publication Data
Nettleton, Pamela Hill.
  William Shakespeare : playwright and poet / by Pamela Hill Nettleton.
    p. cm. — (Signature lives)
  Includes bibliographical references and index.
  ISBN-13: 978-0-7565-0816-6 (hardcover)
  ISBN-10: 0-7565-0816-9 (hardcover)
  ISBN-13: 978-0-7565-1062-6 (paperback)
  ISBN-10: 0-7565-1062-7 (paperback)
  1. Shakespeare, William, 1564–1616—Juvenile literature. 2. Authors,
English—Early modern, 1500–1700—Juvenile literature. I. Title. II.
Series.
  PR2895.N48 2005
  822.3'3—dc22   2004023081

Signature Lives

RENAISSANCE ERA

The Renaissance was a cultural movement that started in Italy in the early 1300s. The word *renaissance* comes from a Latin word meaning "rebirth," and during this time, Europe experienced a rebirth of interest and achievement in the arts, science, and global exploration. People reacted against the religion-centered culture of the Middle Ages to find greater value in the human world. By the time the Renaissance came to a close, around 1600, people had come to look at their world in a brand new way.

William Shakespeare

Table of Contents

1 ALL THE WORLD'S A STAGE

ϲ⌒ᨒᢱᣚ

It is afternoon in London, England, and a crowd is making its way toward a large, round building in the heart of the bustling city. The flag waving atop the roof announces the reason for their visit: a play will be performed today. Paying a penny each, theatergoers cross under the arch and into the open courtyard. The wealthy can pay more for a seat under the roof. The stage sticks out into the middle of the courtyard, and people crush up against one another on three sides for a closer look. As a trumpeter blows his horn, the crowd falls silent. The show is about to start.

William Shakespeare, the famous playwright, poet, and actor, owns this theater, and he is waiting just off stage. This early 17th century crowd, filled

Romeo and Juliet part in this illustration of a famous scene from one of Shakespeare's most popular plays.

with merchants, laborers, artists, students, writers, and even nobles, stands just feet from the man many today consider the greatest writer in the English language.

William Shakespeare was the greatest playwright in the world, and yet his background was not very different from the commonfolk who came to see his plays. Shakespeare wrote plays that are studied in colleges and universities, yet he only had a basic grammar school education. Today's most famous movie stars and greatest actors find Shakespearean roles the most demanding and difficult to play, yet Shakespeare wrote his plays for the people of London who jeered and laughed and cried during performances.

There are many things that are not known about William Shakespeare's life and times. Because records of daily life were not kept in the manner they are today, no one will ever be able to be sure about many aspects of his life—why he made this decision or that one. His plays, however, show us that Shakespeare was a keen observer of the people around him and the various situations in which he found himself in life.

Shakespeare wrote funny comedies, violent tragedies, and human history plays of the famous kings and wars of England. Shakespeare watched how people behaved and how they treated each

Theater was a popular form of entertainment in Shakespeare's time, and townspeople flocked to performances.

other, and he thought hard about what made them act that way. The characters that he made up feel very real because he based them on what he knew about real people in his life. He translated everyday life, as well as the stories of kings and queens, into plays everyone could relate to. As he wrote in one of his plays, "All the world's a stage, And all the men

A statue of William Shakespeare sits in the village of Stratford the birthplace and burial site of the English playwright and poet.

and women merely players."

In addition to observing the people around him, many historians believe that much of Shakespeare's work was based on things that happened in his own life. They suggest that he must have felt love deeply, because he wrote with such joy about young love.

They suggest that the reason audiences feel so strongly for Hamlet after the loss of his father was that Shakespeare was writing from his own loss—the death of his son. They believe that he must have had a wonderful sense of humor, because even his darkest plays often have moments that make audiences laugh.

The lines he wrote are in old language that sometimes sounds funny to us until we get used to it—but once that happens, we hear the truth in his words. Centuries before there were such things as therapists and counselors, Shakespeare understood people. Young lovers in the 21st century can watch *Romeo and Juliet* and know that a writer living 400 years ago knew their feelings and expressed them for all to understand. Children can watch *King Lear* and know that Shakespeare understood the frustration of trying to help an aging parent. We hear Hamlet grieve for his dead father in *Hamlet* or hear Petruchio tease Kate in *The Taming of the Shrew*, and we feel we are in the company of friends.

Though Shakespeare's language is the language of his time, not ours, it speaks from the heart and it touches us. Shakespeare's choices of words and the way he used them express feelings we all have but sometimes have trouble saying. Shakespeare says it for us. ✍

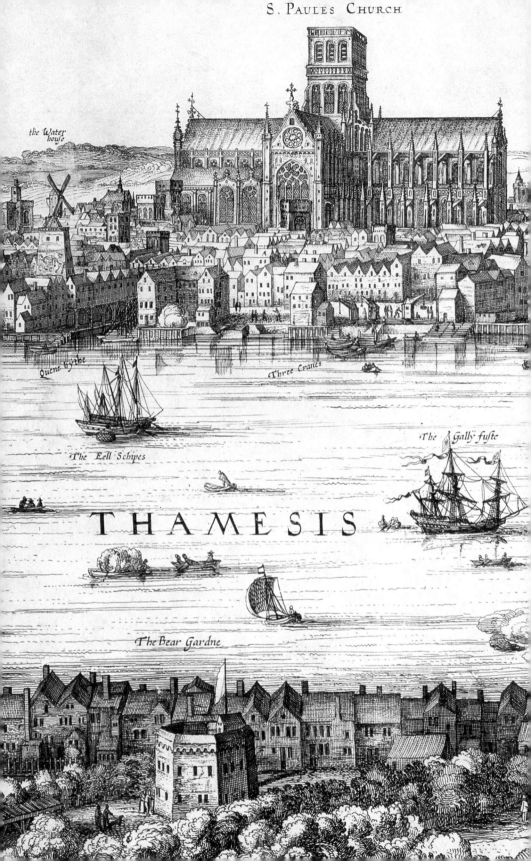

Chapter

2 SHAKESPEARE'S TIME

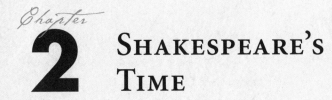

William Shakespeare was born in a time before electricity, television, shopping malls, and cars. Children played by candlelight. Mothers cooked dinner over big fireplaces inside little houses, and fathers farmed land and grew crops or worked at trades like candlemaking or printing.

Homes and restaurants called taverns were often dirty places that were rarely cleaned. There were no refrigerators to keep food from spoiling. People seldom took baths or washed their clothes, so they smelled bad and sometimes even had fleas living on them. All this helped germs flourish and diseases spread. People often got sick or even died from eating bad food or catching diseases. Instead of living into their 70s, 80s, or even 90s the

Sixteenth-century London was a bustling port on the Thames River.

way people do today, Shakespeare's friends and neighbors considered 50 to be old age.

The shortened life span was due in large part to the lack of advancement in medicine at the time. Illnesses were especially common among children, and it was typical that a family would have one child or more die at a very young age. Many children did not live past the age of 5, in part because the immunizations that children routinely receive today did not exist at the time. Those who did become sick were subject to the most basic care. Seeking medical treatment often meant having a portion of one's blood drained from the body. Being "bled" was believed to get rid of the toxins in the body. Unfortunately, people who were weakened by illness often became more seriously ill or died as a result of the bleeding.

The worst illness of the times was the bubonic plague. The bubonic plague tormented Europe from about 1348 to the 1690s. Germs for the plague were carried on fleas that lived on black rats, and since many people kept their garbage right outside their door, these rats ran everywhere—even

Herbs were often used to treat the symptoms of various illnesses. For head pains, physicians would administer sweet-smelling herbs such as rose, lavender, sage, and bay leaf. Stomach pains were treated with wormwood, mint, and balm. For lung problems, patients were given licorice and comfrey. Vinegar was believed to kill disease, and so it was regularly used as a general-purpose cleansing agent.

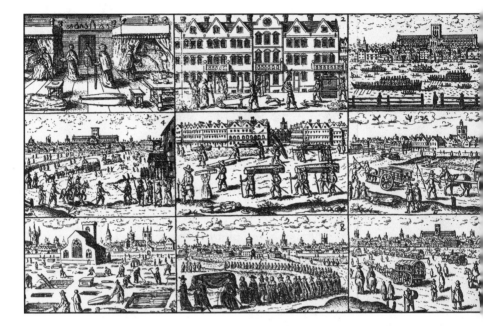

An engraving shows the various stages as the plague devastates a town.

inside houses. The plague gave people a fever, chills, and black, painful bumps under the arms and on the sides of the neck. A person who caught the disease was almost certain to die, and it was so contagious that most of that person's family and friends would become infected and die as well.

Entire towns and villages perished all at once from this terrible disease. So many people died at once that men drove wagons down the streets collecting bodies. "Bring out your dead," they would call, and the family would carry out anyone who died during the night. Bodies were buried in large, group burial sites. During the year 1625, one-fifth of the entire population of England died of the plague.

In Shakespeare's time, people did not understand as much about disease as they do now. They did not know that the plague was caused by the fleas carried by black rats. No one knew for sure how to stop the plague, but they did believe it was contagious. So they passed laws that stopped people from gathering in large groups. As Shakespeare grew up, this law would become very important because it would temporarily close the theaters where his plays could be performed and force him to write poetry to survive.

The plague eventually came to an end when brown rats took over the places where black rats ate and lived. Plague-carrying fleas did not live on brown rats, so as brown rats became dominant, the plague lost its grip on Europe. People of Shakespeare's time did not understand this relationship, and they believed the end of the plague was magical or a sign from God.

People in Shakespeare's time believed many things to be signs from God. They also believed that the theater might be evil. Some people enjoyed the theater, but to others, it was against their religion to attend plays. Later in Shakespeare's life, when one of his theaters burned down, some people thought it was God's way of telling them that plays and theaters were bad.

And yet Shakespeare lived during a time of great progress and growth. He was born during the reign of Queen Elizabeth I, a time that has come to be known as the Elizabethan Era. There were many developments in art and science, and Europeans were pushing back the boundaries of the known world through exploration of the land, the sea, and even the heavens.

Despite all of the advances in knowledge, there was also religious persecution. Queen Elizabeth was an Anglican, and the head of the Church of England. She supported the torture and even killing of Roman Catholics. Though there is some evidence that Shakespeare's father was a Roman Catholic or had Catholic leanings, this was kept secret from the neighbors and friends, probably because of persecution and prejudice against Catholics. Publicly, the Shakespeare family belonged to the Church of England, the state church. ✑

Elizabeth I was crowned queen of England at age 25. She reigned for 45 years.

Francis S. Walker

Chapter
3 SHAKESPEARE AS A BOY

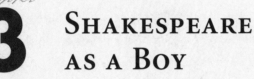

Although Shakespeare spent his life writing, much about his life was never written down. In England in the 1500s and 1600s, when Shakespeare lived, written records were not commonly kept. We do know some things about Shakespeare for certain. For example, William Shakespeare, one of the greatest writers of all time, was born to parents who could not read or write.

William's mother, Mary Arden, was the daughter of a farmer, but she was related to a family of high social standing in the area. Although she could not read or write, that was common for the time. Very few women of her time were literate, and none of them attended school. If a girl could read, it was because her father or brother taught her at home.

Shakespeare grew up in the town of Stratford, England, which was located on the river Avon.

William's father, John Shakespeare, had grown up on a farm and never attended school, either. He made gloves, aprons, and other items out of leather. He also sold wool and perhaps farm products, and he served for many years on the town council. Before his marriage, it appears that John Shakespeare was having some success in business, since he had purchased two additional homes.

When people were married in Shakespeare's day, the new wife often brought with her a dowry—land and money from the bride's father that became the property of the newly married couple. Mary's dowry was ample, and it added to John's status in Stratford. For the next few years, John was one of his town's leaders, moving up to progressively more important offices in local government.

Yet even though he eventually became mayor of his town, Stratford, John Shakespeare signed his name with a mark because he did not even know how to write his name.

John Shakespeare and Mary Arden married in about 1557. Five years later, William was born. The exact date of William's birth is not known, but church records say that he was baptized on April 26, 1564, at Holy Trinity Church in Stratford, England. This tells us that he was probably born in April, and perhaps just a few days before this ceremony. According to the custom at that time, infants were baptized about three days after their birth, so historians generally name the date of Shakepeare's birth as April 23, 1564.

William was the third of eight children born to John and Mary Shakespeare, but he was the oldest child to survive to adulthood. In Shakespeare's time, there were no hospitals or good medical care, so many babies did not live long. William's two older sisters both died as babies. His sister Anne died at age 7. But his three younger brothers—Gilbert, Richard, and Edmund—and one younger sister, Joan, lived to adulthood. William was lucky to live himself.

The parish register of Stratford's Holy Trinity Church lists the dates of both Shakespeare's christening and his burial.

When he was less than 3 months old, the bubonic plague came to Stratford, and one of the Shakespeares' neighbors lost all four of their children to the disease. William's family was lucky, however. No one in his family died from the plague.

The Shakespeare family lived on Henley Street in Stratford, a small town about 75 miles (120 kilometers) northwest of London in a part of England called Warwickshire. Because the town is on the river Avon, it is sometimes called Stratford-Upon-Avon, or Stratford-on-Avon.

The man who built the bridge over the Avon River, Sir Hugh Clopton, built a large house in Stratford that he called New Place. Later, when William was a success in the theater world, he bought New Place, and his family lived there.

A stone bridge crossed the river Avon at Stratford, and travelers and merchants who used the bridge brought traffic and business, helping the town thrive.

When William was about 4 years old, his father became mayor of Stratford. Although John Shakespeare served for only one term, he remained a town leader for many years, and the Shakespeares became an important family in Stratford.

In England during that time, there were very specific classes of people. Children were born into whatever class their parents belonged. Royalty or nobles, such as lords and ladies, belonged to the highest class. Peasants, the poor, and the uneducated made up the lower classes. In between were people like the Shakespeare family.

Shakespeare spent his entire life in England, and probably only lived in two towns.

As John Shakespeare became more successful in his business, he applied to the College of Arms asking for something that was very important in England—a coat of arms. A coat of arms is a design made for just one family. The design often looks like a shield or a banner and has items in it that are meaningful for the family. For example, if the family raised sheep and lived in the hills, perhaps their coat of arms would include a sheep and a hillside. This design was used on doors, clothing, flags, and household goods. When a family had a coat of arms, that meant they were of a higher class.

Shakespeare's birthplace still stands in Stratford and continues to draw many tourists.

If John Shakespeare could buy a coat of arms for his family, he would help advance them in the

class system. He applied in 1569, but his request was denied.

There are many things that are not known about Shakespeare's young life, but historians are able to draw some conclusions based on what we do know about him in later years. For example, some historians suggest that Shakespeare must have been close to his mother and sisters, because his treatment of women in his plays was generally very favorable. Women of the day were often portrayed as being needy or frail, but Shakespeare's women are typically strong-willed, confident, and likeable. Even when his female characters do bad or mischievous things, the audience generally understands why and has a positive feeling about the character. ⬱

4 AT SCHOOL AND BEYOND

༄

There are no written records of William attending school. However, one of the first people to write about Shakespeare's life, Nicholas Rowe, said that William did attend a school. It was probably the King's New School near his home in Stratford.

Like all schools in Shakespeare's time, the King's New School was for boys only. He probably began his studies there at the age of 7.

School was a long day for boys like William. Classes started at 6 A.M. and continued until dinnertime at about 6 P.M. Each day began and ended with Protestant Devotions. School met six days a week, every week, without holidays or vacations. Teachers were strict, and students were physically punished if they broke the rules. The boys learned addition and

A painting by Dutch artist David Teniers (the elder) shows a 16th-century village fair, much like the ones that came to Stratford in Shakespeare's time.

subtraction, the alphabet, and Latin. At the time, knowing Latin, the language of ancient Rome, was a sign of an educated person. It was also the language needed for a career in medicine, law, and religion. Students also learned many Anglican prayers, lessons, and psalms. They read the great literary classics and studied Aesop's Fables. As an older student, William probably read classical writers such as Cicero, Virgil, and Ovid. William's love of these classics shows up years later in many of the plots of plays he wrote as an adult.

Shakespeare's education was not considered a "classical education." Still, students of his time were given basic rhetorical training. This meant that they were taught to consider all sides of a situation in order to be able to make a fair and impartial judgment. This training shows through in much of Shakespeare's work. Whether the play is a comedy or tragedy, whether there are two main characters or 10, Shakespeare was able to help the audience see the point of view of each of them. This allows the audience to understand why certain characters act in certain ways, regardless of whether they are "good" or "bad."

Along with school, William also attended church catechism classes, plus Mass and other services. William clearly received specific education in the Bible; some of the themes and stories told in the Bible are echoed in his own work in his later years. Most people of Shakespeare's time read the Bible and studied its teachings, so using biblical stories as a framework for his plays helped Shakespeare

Shakespeare probably attended the King's New School.

reach his audience with familiar material in a recognizable format.

By the time William was about 13, his father was struggling to make enough money for his family. The business was not going well, and John Shakespeare was having trouble paying his bills. In addition, he often went out of his way to help others, sometimes literally at his own expense. For example, John often agreed to back up the loans of other members of the community. This meant that if the borrower could not repay the loan, John Shakespeare would have to bear the burden of repayment. He began to accumulate a great deal of debt, and eventually was unable to get out from under the financial strain. The impact of John Shakespeare's financial troubles must have been great on William. It may have later prompted him to advise, in his play *Hamlet*, "Neither a borrower nor a lender be."

As a result of John Shakespeare's financial troubles, there was not enough money to continue to send William to school and on to college. At this time, however, it was common for boys of William's age to leave home and live with a master craftsman as an apprentice in order to learn a trade. Though no records prove this happened, it is possible that William's father took him out of school to teach him to work with leather in the glove-making trade.

Of course, as with most things in William

Shakespeare's early life, there are no records to prove that William was ever apprenticed to his father in any way. In fact, there are no written records at all between his baptism in 1564 and his marriage. So what was William Shakespeare doing?

We can learn some things from his plays. For example, William writes as though he knows a great deal about the law. So perhaps he worked as a clerk in a lawyer's office. In several plays, he writes about butchery, so he may have helped slaughter animals or tan hides.

Since the leather for gloves comes from the skin of animals, William's father may have also butchered

A butcher's shop from the time of Shakespeare

animals. In doing so, however, he would have been breaking the rules of the town. Tradesmen followed specific guidelines about what they could and could not do. Though butchery was connected to making leather, a glover was not supposed to also be a butcher. Still, young William may have learned how to butcher animals, since the plays he wrote as an adult indicate he knew his way around a butcher's shop.

There is a story, which may or may not be true, that helps explain what Shakespeare might have done between leaving school and getting married. According to the story, Shakespeare was sent out of town for poaching a deer from a local squire. English landowners owned all the animals on their property, and it was considered a serious crime for anyone else to kill a rabbit, deer, or any animal, on the landowner's property, even if the person used it to feed his family. This crime, called poaching, was punishable in many ways, one of which was being sent away from home.

He might also have worked for a time as a live-in schoolteacher at the home of a wealthy family friend. If so, he may have seen plays performed in the house's great hall by traveling troupes of actors. This might have been his first exposure to acting and stage plays.

One of the events English villagers looked forward to was a town fair. Farmers sold crops, and

merchants sold items such as cloth, baskets, and furniture. Fairs always had lots of things to eat. Sometimes there would also be jugglers, magicians, or dancers. Sometimes there would even be plays.

In a time without modern transportation, people could not travel to a theater. So, actors traveled to their audience. Actors, playwrights, directors, and costumers banded together in groups

An engraving depicts the legend in which the young Shakespeare is brought before a landowner for the crime of poaching and is sent away from home.

Traveling theater companies would often perform in the yard of neighborhood taverns.

called acting companies. They loaded up wagons with costumes, makeup, and props, and rode around the countryside, putting on shows outdoors, at fairs, in taverns, and in the large houses that belonged to members of the upper class.

For actors to make any money, a wealthy nobleman or a king or queen had to support them with money and places to perform. When actors stopped at the large country houses of nobles to perform plays, all the people who worked at the great house—gardeners, cooks, maids, and nannies, as well as their family and friends—gathered to watch the play. Sometimes the company acted out stories, such as the tales of Robin Hood and his Merry Men. Sometimes actors recited long, sad poems or sang ballads.

An acting company probably had 10 to 12 members, all of whom were men. There were never women in acting companies. At that time, it was considered indecent for women to be on stage.

The companies traveled in covered wagons, and some actors rode horses. A few would ride on ahead to a town and ask the mayor for permission to perform there. They had the best luck if a local nobleman would loan them livery, a name for special uniforms of the people who worked for the gentry.

The plays were exciting, but the actors themselves fascinated townspeople. Most villagers traveled no more than a few miles from their homes during their lifetime, yet actors rode from town to town across England. Actors in Shakespeare's time were like today's movie and rock stars. People were interested in how they spoke, dressed, and behaved.

Perhaps, during this time, William saw a traveling troupe of players and thought about going to London to act in plays. He might have even thought about writing them. There are many stories, but no proof of what really happened. That is, until 1582.

Delen McC... 1700

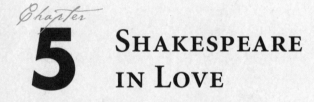

5 SHAKESPEARE IN LOVE

Chapter

❦

In 1582, Shakespeare married Anne Hathaway, the daughter of a farmer from the nearby village of Shottery. Shakespeare was 18 years old, and Anne was 26.

Anne's father had just died, leaving Anne alone with her stepmother and three stepbrothers. It could be that Anne was eager to leave home, and the young William Shakespeare offered an opportunity to begin a different life.

In the fall of 1582, she told friends of her father that she was pregnant and that Shakespeare was the father. Farmer Hathaway's friends may have gone to the Shakespeare home, knocked on the door, and talked seriously to William Shakespeare and his father. They may have forced him to marry Anne.

A drawing is thought to be a portrait of William Shakespeare's wife, Anne Hathaway.

Regardless, the marriage of Anne Hathaway and William Shakespeare was unusual in a number of ways. During this time, few marriages were the result of a young couple falling in love and seeking to start a future together. Marriage was a very businesslike arrangement. The bride's dowry was a major consideration, and the couple was often not even in love. Parents of the couple were often involved in selecting an appropriate—and profitable— match for their children.

Also, men typically didn't marry until they reached their mid-20s, and then it was generally to a younger woman. At that point, the men would typically be in good financial position to provide for a new family.

So Shakespeare's marriage to a woman eight years older than himself seems out of place for the time. Shakespeare's work may offer some explanation. His plays are full of stories of the joys of young love, so many scholars believe that he and Anne must have been in love.

Aside from the age difference, Anne would have been con-

Some scholars have suggested that there was some animosity between the Hathaway and Shakespeare families— a theory that is supported by Shakespeare's work. Shakespeare wrote of the dangers of families interfering in the fates of young lovers, most notably in Romeo and Juliet, *in which two young lovers struggle to find happiness together in the midst of a war between their families.*

Anne Hathaway lived in a cottage in Shottery, England, before her marriage to Shakespeare.

sidered a good match for William. She was from the same social class and was able to provide enough of a dowry to improve the couple's financial standing after the marriage.

On November 28, 1582, a court document authorized the marriage. The wedding probably happened within days. Susanna, their daughter, was born five months later and was christened on May 26, 1583.

There are no records of what Shakespeare did to earn money, or even of where he and Anne lived in the early years of their marriage. Since they had little money of their own, he may have taken her home to live with his parents on Henley Street. Shakespeare's mother might have helped Anne with baby Susanna while raising his brothers and sister, who were 16, 13, 8, and 2 years old.

In the winter of 1585, Anne and Shakespeare had two more children—twins named Hamnet and Judith—who they named after friends who lived nearby. When friends Hamnet and Judith Sadler had their own son, they named him William in return.

If, at this time, William knew he wanted to be a writer, he would have had a hard time finding work in Stratford. A small village like Stratford had no jobs for a writer. In those days, published books were rare and too expensive for anyone but the richest people to buy. Still, he must have worked somewhere to support his little family.

Perhaps he helped his father out in the shop. Perhaps he overheard tales of London and life in a big city when he visited the local tavern. And perhaps he started to make plans to travel to London.

Many scholars who study Shakespeare refer to the years between 1585, when the twins were bap-

tized, and 1592, when he was first mentioned as a playwright in London, as "the lost years." Although no real factual information exists on Shakespeare's life for this period, scholars have offered lots of ideas about what Shakespeare might have been doing during this time.

Since his father's financial situation was not good, William may have helped out with his father's business. Because some of his later work reflects a great deal of knowledge about horses, there are some historians who believe he took care of the

An English engraving shows the Shakespeare family at the time he was a successful playwright.

> *In Shakespeare's time, the theater was the only real mass entertainment able to convey ideas and information to a large audience. The Queen's Men acting company was organized to deliver the queen's messages to her people in the form of entertainment. Through their performances, the troupe reinforced the belief that the queen stood for good and those who opposed her rule would meet with a terrible end.*

horses of the people of nobility who visited Stratford. Some even suggest that he may have traveled to Italy during this time, as his work shows a great deal of knowledge about that country.

Regardless of his profession at the time, Shakespeare was most likely infatuated by the theater and attended the plays performed by the traveling groups that visted Stratford. It may have been with one of these acting companies that he got his "big chance" in theater.

One popular theory about Shakespeare's lost years has to do with a traveling troupe of actors that visited Stratford in 1587. These actors were called the Queen's Men, because Queen Elizabeth I was their patron. One of the actors had recently been killed in a bar quarrel, and when the troupe arrived in Stratford, they were one actor short. Shakespeare might have stepped in to help.

At this time, Shakespeare was 23 years old and the father of three children. He may have been living at home with his parents. He might have felt restless. He might have felt eager to travel and see more of the world. Joining the Queen's Men might have satisfied a number of yearnings. And if he didn't join The Queen's Men, perhaps he joined another group of actors. Of course, there are no records that tell us what happened, but it makes for a good story.

In 1588, Shakespeare's name appears in a Stratford lawsuit. His parents' names appear as well. However, Shakespeare may not have been living in Stratford any more. Whether he left with the Queen's Men, another acting company, or on his own, scholars believe that some time during these "lost years" Shakespeare moved to London, leaving his family behind.

Were Shakespeare and Anne mad at other and did they separate? Did they wish they had never gotten married? Historians can only wonder. At some point, he wrote Anne a silly poem making a joke out of how her name, Hathaway, sounds like "hate away." It is Sonnet 145.

One way or another, by 1592, Shakespeare had left Stratford, Anne, and the children while he went to London, the center of theater life. ✑

6 SHAKESPEARE IN LONDON

Chapter

❦

London during Shakespeare's time was an exciting place to be. With a population of nearly 200,000, it was an active, crowded city, as well as one of the world's chief trading and commercial centers. London was also the capital of England and home of the queen and her court. Artists, musicians, writers, and actors traveled to London to seek their fortune. Shakespeare was one of these fortune-seekers.

When Shakespeare arrived in London, there were three main theaters where townspeople could see plays: the Swan, the Rose, and Burbage's Theatre. The young Shakespeare may have found work at one or more of these theaters.

Each theater had a resident acting company, and both theater and company were run by a small

A portrait of Shakespeare shows the young actor and play-wright with a skull, an item commonly added to portraits of the time to remind people of the temporary nature of life.

group of owners. These owners were also usually the company's leading actors. However, there were a variety of other jobs with theater companies as well. Theaters needed people to "park" the horses of audience members. Actors needed prompters to sit in the wings and whisper cues to them if they forgot their lines. A prompter, like an understudy, might now and then even have to take the place of an actor, and might eventually even become a regular actor in the company.

The dozen men and boys who made up each theater company worked very hard. They put on a different play each day, six days a week, and they memorized about 800 lines for each one. Young boys apprenticed to theater companies. They ran errands, carried costumes, and moved scenery. Boys

London's many theaters flew flags on their roofs to show that a play would be performed that day.

between the ages of 10 and 15 whose voices hadn't changed yet also had another job—they played the parts of women since women were not allowed on stage.

At first, Shakespeare probably acted in small parts, but eventually he took on more prominent roles, and before long he was acting in his own plays. Some evidence suggests that he went bald at an early age. This gave him an unusual advantage as an actor because it allowed him to play the parts of older men. Once Shakespeare was working in a theater company, it would have been easy for him to write plays for the company to perform.

We know that by 1592 Shakespeare had not only joined an acting company, but was also writing plays for the company, because a pamphlet published that year refers to Shakespeare as a playwright and actor. In this pamphlet, the author refers to Shakespeare as "Shake-scene," because of his thundering voice and his vivid and dramatic writing. The author also accuses Shakespeare of thinking that he, an uneducated actor, could write as well as a university-educated playwright.

Although he may not have been university edu-

> *Actors often didn't memorize their lines exactly. They would improvise or make up their lines as they went along. Each time the play was performed, it would be slightly different. The most important thing for actors to remember was when to enter or exit the stage.*

cated, Shakespeare was on the rise as a playwright. During his time, plays that dealt with historical topics were very popular. People loved to see plays about the royalty of England and Europe. Stories about who killed whom and which armies triumphed brought in the crowds. And so Shakespeare wrote these types of plays—called history plays.

But *how* he wrote them was different. The characters in history plays were usually rather wooden, and the plots were boring. What happened to the kings and queens was usually blamed on destiny. This made the characters powerless, so none of the action seemed that exciting. Shakespeare took a different approach. He made the historic generals and kings into real-life people who had flaws and made mistakes like everyone else. He showed how their faults and feelings drove their decisions and directed the course of history.

Traditionally, Shakespeare's plays have been divided into three groups: histories, comedies, and tragedies. In general, he focused on a different kind of play at different points in his career, and his career is often thought of in four parts. Many of his early plays were history plays, because such plays were popular at the time.

The plays of Shakespeare's first period, which covers the years 1590 through 1594, were largely based on Roman authors and English historians.

But even with his other types of plays, Shakespeare followed the Elizabethan custom of basing his plots on existing historical and literary works. Yet although he borrowed the storyline, he changed the telling, adding his own wit and flair to the language.

Shakespeare's troupe was often invited to perform before the queen and her court.

Shakespeare's first history plays were three plays in a series about England's King Henry VI. Ned Allyn, the leading actor of the time, played the lead. These plays tell the story of one period of British royal history with lots of blood, wars, violence, and murder. These three plays were followed some years later by four additional "Henry Plays," as they are often called. Other plays in the series include two about Henry IV, one about Henry V, and one about Henry VIII.

Another early play was *Titus Andronicus*, a particularly violent story that has Titus grinding his enemy's bones into flour and using it to make a pie! Audiences loved it.

Other plays from this period include the comedies *The Comedy of Errors*, *The Taming of the Shrew*, and *The Two Gentlemen of Verona*, and the histories *Richard III* and *King John*.

Shakespeare was unusual among playwrights of his time in that he wrote only for his own acting company. The parts he created were written to suit the strengths of particular actors. Because he was also associated with a particular theater, he wrote with the building's features in mind as well.

Theater buildings in Shakespeare's time were different from those of today. Although there were smaller, private theaters for the upper class that had roofs and artificial lighting, most theaters in his time were public

Unlike today, theaters in Shakespeare's time had no scenery and few props. The play's setting was often established in its opening lines, rather than through a set. Acting companies, however, often used elaborate costumes, music, acrobats, and special effects, such as stage cannons.

theaters. These public theaters had no artificial lighting, so plays could only be performed during the daylight hours. They were also built around a courtyard that had no roof. As a result, plays could only be performed in the warmer months.

Francis Wheatly's painting shows a scene from Shakespeare's comedy The Taming of the Shrew.

At one end of the courtyard was a stage, which projected into the courtyard. On the other end and continuing along the sides were three levels of seating, called galleries. The price of admission bought one standing room in the courtyard, but wealthier

A typical Elizabethan theater had a stage, galleries, and courtyard.

theatergoers could pay extra to sit in the galleries. The stage had a main level in front and an upper level at the back. A small half roof, usually made of straw, covered the upper stage and some of the main stage. Among other things, the stage itself was equipped with a trap door. This made it possible for actors playing the roles of ghosts or spirits to rise from the grave.

By 1592, Shakespeare had written between five and seven plays. But he did not record the dates he composed them, so it is hard to know exactly when each was written.

Shakespeare also didn't worry about the scripts at all. He gave the actors copies of their lines, but he did not gather together his plays and think of publishing them. Publishing plays was not something people did in the 1500s. Plays were fun to write. They were fun to perform. But playwrights weren't serious writers. Serious writers of the time wrote books and poetry.

Although a number of Shakespeare's plays were printed during his lifetime, he had very little to do with their publication. Publishing in this era was very difficult and expensive, because the printing press, which could mass-produce printed materials, was still very new. Also, the cost of materials, especially paper, was very high. In addition, Shakespeare was probably influenced by his own actors, who did not want his works to be published. They were worried that if the plays were published, other acting companies would

Even though Shakespeare never published his own work, some other theater groups did attempt to produce his plays. However, these troupes never achieved the same level of success with them that Shakespeare's acting company did.

Shakespeare wrote plays to suit the actors of his own troupe, including the comic actor Will Kempe (right)

begin to perform them, and Shakespeare's troupe would not make as much money. By keeping them to themselves, only they could perform the plays. And as Shakespeare's fame grew, this became even more important.

However, in 1591, London's focus turned away from the theater. The bubonic plague was striking the city and lingered there into 1593, sometimes killing 1,000 people a week. Throughout the city, people were contracting the deadly disease, which could bring death in as little as three days. It was highly contagious, so it had a more devastating impact on the poor, who lived in less sanitary conditions. By this time, Shakespeare had been successful enough that his living conditions were fairly good, and so he wasn't in as much danger as others who were less fortunate.

Still, London was not a good place to be, even for the wealthy. Many of the healthy attempted to flee the city in order to avoid contracting the disease, but people who lived on the outskirts of town were not willing to take them in, fearing they might actually be ill.

Many of the deeply religious Puritans felt that God was responsible for the plague and that the people of London were being punished for their "sinful" ways. Among the things they blamed as sinful was the theater. They believed the theaters were full of bad behavior. In part because of the Puritans' beliefs, and in part because large gatherings were likely to expose more people to the plague, performances in theaters were outlawed in 1592.

Throughout all of this, Shakespeare's writing was not slowed. He stayed in London and continued his writing, turning his focus to poetry. ❧

Chapter 7 SHAKESPEARE'S POEMS

❧❀❧

Even with no novels, movies, or television, people in the 1500s loved a good story. This is one reason plays were so popular. Plays allowed people to enjoy a great story while at the same time often learning something about the history of England or about the world.

And yet people of this time considered plays to be a lesser form of art than poetry. A poet did important work, while a playwright was often thought to simply be "playing." So, while the theaters were closed because of the plague, Shakespeare found another way to tell his stories. He wrote two long poems. *Venus and Adonis* was published in 1593, and *The Rape of Lucrece* was published in 1594. These poems, called narratives, told stories from mythology and

A painting by John James Chalon shows Shakespeare reading before Queen Elizabeth I and her court.

> *During Shakespeare's time, stories were also told through songs. Singers traveled to fairs and great houses around the countryside, singing long songs called ballads about great achievements and heroes of the time.*

history that Shakespeare probably studied in school.

In Shakespeare's day, poets often addressed their writing to one person. This was almost always some noble person, such as a lord or a prince, who could give the poet money for the poems. Sometimes nobles hired poets to write, and sometimes poets just addressed work to nobles, hoping they'd like the poems and then pay for them. Shakespeare dedicated both *Venus and Adonis* and *The Rape of Lucrece* to the 19-year-old Earl of Southhampton, most likely with the hope of receiving a financial reward.

Some scholars believe that Shakespeare may have first become acquainted with the earl in his younger days, when Shakespeare tended the horses of nobles who were attending plays. They suggest that Shakespeare became a well-liked attendant of the rich and powerful and that these wealthy nobles sought him out personally to watch their horses during performances. Shakespeare may have then used these relationships to help him further his career as a playwright and poet.

In dedicating *Venus and Adonis* to the Earl of Southhampton, Shakespeare wrote:

I know not how I shall offend in dedicating my unpolished lines to your Lordship, nor how the world will censure me for choosing so strong a prop to support so weak a burden; only if your Honour seem but pleased, I account myself highly praised, and vow to take advantage of all idle hours, till I have honoured you with some graver labour.

A woodcut of the opening of Shakespeare's 1593 narrative poem, Venus and Adonis

VENUS AND ADONIS.

EVEN AS THE SUNNE WITH PUR-PLE-COL-OURD FACE, HAD TANE HIS LAST LEAVE OF THE WEEP-ING MORNE,
ROSE-CHEEKT ADONIS HIED HIM TO THE CHACE,
HUNTING HE LOV'D, BUT LOVE HE LAUGHT TO SCORNE:
SICK-THOUGHTED VENUS MAKES AMAINE UNTO HIM,
AND LIKE A BOLD FAC'D SUTER GINNES TO WOO HIM.

THRISE FAIRER THEN MY SELFE, (THUS SHE BEGAN)
THE FIELDS CHIEFE FLOWER, SWEET ABOVE COMPARE,
STAINE TO ALL NIMPHS, MORE LOVELY THEN A MAN,
MORE WHITE, AND RED, THEN DOVES, OR ROSES ARE:

In his dedication, Shakespeare wrote with a humble tone; by calling his work "unpolished lines," Shakespeare was making sure the earl knew that he was modest about the quality of his own work. He also made an offer to provide the earl with more poetry if the earl was pleased with what he read. In fact, Shakespeare made a plea to become the earl's personal poet. Offering to "take advantage of all idle hours" is Shakespeare's way of saying that he will work tirelessly to write in a way that will make the earl happy.

Apparently, the plea worked. Scholars believe that Shakespeare received money from the earl that he later used to invest in a theater company. The dedication of his later narrative, *The Rape of Lucrece*, seems to express gratitude to the earl, as if Shakespeare is thanking the earl for supporting his work.

Shakespeare's clever handling of the rich and noble would serve him well throughout his life. In later years, he became a favorite of kings and queens, and his career grew dramatically.

In Shakespeare's time, paper was very expensive. The sheets of paper he needed to write one play would have cost Shakespeare all the money he could earn in a month. To write on this paper, he probably used a quill pen made of a large bird feather. Shakespeare had a reputation for never changing lines once he wrote them down. Like the composer Mozart, who lived more than a hundred years later, Shakespeare was known for writing nearly perfect versions of his work in the first draft.

A recently discovered poem is written in Shakespeare's own handwriting.

Shakespeare's narrative poems were published and became very popular. They were not published like books today, however. They were published as quartos, sheets of paper printed and then folded into quarters and sold unbound. If you wanted a cover for your little book, you had to make one yourself.

Shakespeare also wrote shorter poems, called sonnets, which follow a specific format. A sonnet always has 14 lines and a specific pattern in which certain lines must rhyme with other lines. For example, if each letter stands for a line

When London's theaters closed because of the plague, Shakespeare continued his career by writing poetry.

that ends in a particular sound (A lines rhyme with other A lines, B lines with other B lines, C with C, etc.), Shakespeare's sonnets were often written in this pattern: ABAB CDCD EFEF GG.

Sonnets are also written so that the accented syllables in the words in the line make a special rhythm. This rhythm is called iambic pentameter. The word *iambic* refers to the placement of the accents. In poetry that follows an iambic pattern, every other syllable is stressed, beginning with an unaccented syllable. *Pentameter* refers to the five iambic groupings that make up a line.

> In Shakespeare's time, spellings of words were not yet firmly established. There were many ways to spell the same word, and many words were spelled differently than they are today. For example, here was sometimes spelled heare, and I could also be written as aye.

Shakespeare wrote 154 sonnets. The first 126 sonnets are addressed to the same person, a rich nobleman. The first dozen sonnets try to convince the young nobleman to get married and have children. Some Shakespeare scholars think that the nobleman's mother may have asked Shakespeare to write these poems.

After the first 12 sonnets, Shakespeare's poems become very loving. Some scholars think perhaps he may have been in love with the young nobleman. Other scholars think that they were simply good

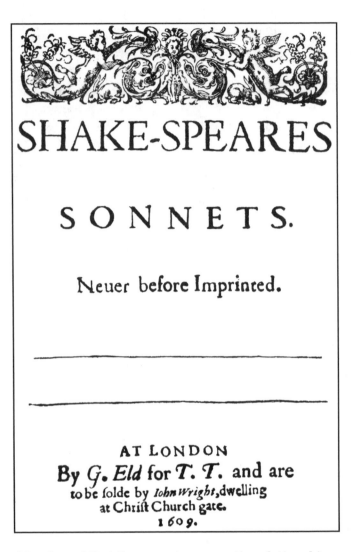

SHAKE-SPEARES

SONNETS.

Neuer before Imprinted.

AT LONDON
By *G. Eld* for *T. T.* and are
to be folde by *Iohn Wright*, dwelling
at Chriſt Church gate.
1 6 0 9.

friends and that it was not a romantic relationship.

The last 28 sonnets are called the "dark lady" poems because they seem to be written to various women. At least one of these sonnets was written to his wife, Anne Hathaway. Others seem to have been written for a woman he calls his mistress—a lady who may not even have existed, or at least whose identity is still unknown. In Shakespeare's day, it was not unusual for married men to have one or more girlfriends. However, when you see the word *mistress* used in old plays, books, and poems, it does not necessarily mean something romantic. Sometimes, the word *mistress* is used simply to refer to a woman.

In 1609, Shakespeare's sonnets were published, although he probably had nothing to do with this. He thought of the poems as private and probably never intended to print them. ℘

Shakespeare used the English language masterfully, but he also expanded English vocabulary by creating new words. In his poems and plays, Shakespeare invented roughly 2,000 new words and expressions, many of which we still use today. They include bandit, moonbeam, mimic, luggage, puke, and leapfrog, as well as "for goodness's sake," "a sorry sight," "in my mind's eye," and "eaten out of house and home."

8 SUCCESS AS A PLAYWRIGHT

Chapter

ʚ⟨∽⟩ɞ

When the plague scare ended in 1594 and the theaters reopened, Shakespeare's acting company, which he ran with two other men, Richard Burbage and William Kempe, returned to the stage. But it had a new name: the Lord Chamberlain's Men. In addition to his duties as an owner and actor, Shakespeare wrote an average of two plays a year for his company.

The reopening of the theaters marks the beginning of what scholars consider to be Shakespeare's second period as a playwright. Between 1594 and 1600, Shakespeare perfected history plays and comedies. Plays from this period include the comedies *A Midsummer Night's Dream, Love's Labours Lost, The Merchant of Venice, As You Like It, Much*

William Shakespeare, now a successful playwright, looks down on the busy streets of London.

> *In Romeo and Juliet,
> written about 1594, the
> title characters fall in
> love, but their families'
> hate for each other
> leads to the young
> lovers' deaths. In 1596's
> A Midsummer Night's
> Dream, the King and
> Queen of the Fairies
> play tricks on each
> other and on human
> lovers in the forest.*

Ado About Nothing, Twelfth Night, and *The Merry Wives of Windsor,* the histories *Richard II, Henry IV,* and *Henry V,* and the tragedies *Romeo and Juliet* and *Julius Caesar.*

Though audiences liked his plays, other writers attacked Shakespeare. Richer and more educated, they made fun of Shakespeare for being a common man who did not even go to a university. They were jealous of Shakespeare's talent as a playwright and of his success in the theater as an actor, producer, playwright, and owner. Shakespeare and the Lord Chamberlain's Men were favorites of the queen, and they were becoming famous and wealthy.

Though Shakespeare is known today for his plays, they were not what made him rich. Shakespeare made his money by owning his acting company, as well as by receiving support from the nobles for whom he wrote his sonnets. He also made money from the sale of his narrative poems.

Once Shakespeare made enough money, he paid to have a coat of arms made for his family. In 1596, at the age of 32, Shakespeare applied to the same

In A Midsummer Night's Dream, *fairies meddle in the lives of human lovers.*

College of Arms that had rejected his father's application. This time, the coat of arms was awarded to the Shakespeares. William had achieved something he knew was very important to his father.

Now Shakespeare had a coat of arms he could pass on to his son. But tragically, on August 11, 1596,

Shakespeare finally was granted the coat of arms his father had sought years before.

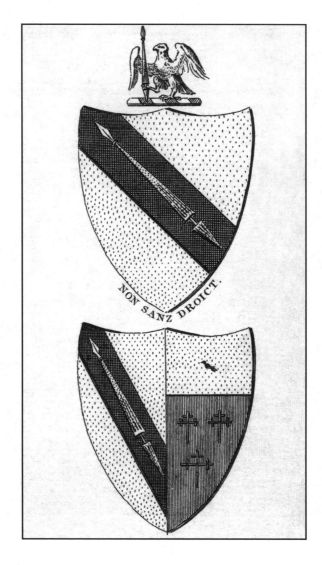

Shakespeare's son Hamnet died. He was only 11 years old. There are no records that tell us whether Hamnet had a long illness or if he died unexpectedly from an accident. Shakespeare wrote many of his sad and tragic plays after his son's death, including

Hamlet, in which he cast himself in the role of the ghost of Hamlet's father. Scholars of Shakespeare believe he used this role to express his grief for his son's death.

By 1598, at least eight of Shakespeare's plays had made their way into print, but not with Shakespeare's consent. Printers of the time could publish and sell anyone's writing without the writer's permission. The writer did not earn any money from the sale of his work. Sometimes, printers put a famous writer's name on another writer's work to help it sell more copies. Printers created and sold their own versions of Shakespeare's plays. These plays circulated throughout London, making Shakespeare's name well known.

About this time, the Lord Chamberlain's Men needed a new theater in which to perform its plays. The company rented the land their theater was built on, and their landlord kept raising the rent. However, they owned the theater structure itself.

Richard Burbage's father James had dreamed of building a new theater outside the area controlled by the conservative Puritans, but he died before his

In 1597, after becoming successful as an actor, theater owner, and playwright, Shakespeare bought his family a large house in Stratford, called New Place. And although he continued to live and work in London, records of business dealings showed he preferred to invest most of his money in his home town.

dream could be fulfilled. Burbage and his brother, Cuthbert, did not want to let their father's dream die as well. They devised a plan in which five members of the acting company—Shakespeare among them—would put up enough money for a new theater in exchange for a share of ownership.

Pooling their money, they quickly made plans to open a theater on the other side of the Thames River. And so, in the dark of night, just like a scene in one of his own plays, Shakespeare and the other owners and actors took apart the building, board by board, and ferried it across the Thames to a new site. There, they rebuilt their theater. They called the new structure the Globe.

The site for the new theater was far from majestic, and the new location forced the majority of theatergoers to take a boat across the Thames in order to attend a play. But the theater quickly became a success. Owning the theater building itself and controlling the land gave Shakespeare's company an important edge over their competitors of the day— they were able to make more money off of their productions than other companies were.

The Globe opened in May of 1599 and held 2,500 to 3,000 people. Probably the first play to open at the Globe was *Henry V.* A line in its opening speech referred to "this wooden O," which meant the shape of the theater.

The Globe was a round building with a similarly shaped interior. And like many theaters of the time, it was built around a courtyard that had no roof. Located in the London suburb of Southwark, the Globe did a booming business and was the most luxurious theater in town. Atop the theater was a flag that bore the crest of the theater: Hercules holding a globe on his shoulders. Depending on the play being performed, other flags may have been raised as well.

The Globe was the finest theater of its day.

Sometimes a flag would be flown that showed an image from the play. Other times, color coding was used. A black flag meant the company would be performing a tragedy, a white flag meant comedy, and a red flag meant a history play.

Above the entrance doors was written a phrase from one of Shakespeare's plays, *Totus mundus agit histrionem*, or "The whole world's a theater." Shakespeare liked this line and wrote an expanded version of it in his play *As You Like It:*

> *All the world's a stage,*
> *And all the men and women*
> *merely players.*
> *They have their exits and*
> *their entrances;*
> *And one man in his time*
> *plays many parts.*

And in *The Merchant of Venice*, he wrote, "I hold the world but as ... a stage, where every man must play a part." These famous lines reflect one of the reasons Shakespeare's writing has been able to touch so many lives. Because he believed that all people were part of an enormous play that was their everyday lives, Shakespeare was able to make the characters he wrote think, feel, and act like real people. Even when writing about kings and queens, Shakespeare differed from other writers of his day.

SCOTLAND Hamlet

Macbeth DENMARK

ENGLAND

E U R O P E

King Lear

Henry V

Atlantic Ocean

FRANCE Taming of the Shrew Othello

Padua Venice
Mantua

NAVARRE Romeo and Juliet

Love's Labours Lost Rome

Julius Caesar

Antony and Cleopatra

Troilus and Cressida

Black Sea

Troy

Othello

GREECE

Messina Athens

Cyprus

Much Ado About Nothing

A Midsummer Night's Dream

Mediterranean Sea

Alexandria

AFRICA

Antony and Cleopatra

0 — 400 miles
0 — 400 kilometers

N W E S

He didn't make them appear all-powerful. Instead, he made certain that audiences understood that even members of the nobility made the same mistakes and shared the same problems of common people. In doing this, he made them more appealing to his audiences and so increased the popularity of his work. ℘

Although he may have never left England, Shakespeare set his plays in many different locations throughout Europe and North Africa.

9 AT THE PEAK OF HIS POWERS

⟨ formatting ⟩

With the opening of the Globe, Shakespeare was even more productive as a playwright, and the great plays of his third period were first produced on the Globe's stage. The third period, from 1601 to 1608, is the time during which Shakespeare wrote his greatest tragedies. *Hamlet, King Lear, Othello, Antony and Cleopatra*, and *Macbeth* are among his most famous and highly regarded works. And yet his masterpieces from this period also include the comedies *All's Well That Ends Well* and *Measure for Measure*.

His later comedies and tragedies were written to highlight the strengths of actors in his company. For example, many of his comedies were written to suit the abilities of his best comic actor, Will Kempe. The later tragedies were written to

A memorable scene from Hamlet, *one of Shakespeare's most famous and well-regarded plays.*

Richard Burbage was one of the Lord Chamberlain's Men's leading actors.

suit Richard Burbage, the company's leading tragic actor. Tragedies such as *Hamlet, Macbeth,* and *King Lear* showed the inner thoughts and feelings of characters in ways that everyone could understand and feel sympathy for. These plays are among Shakespeare's most complex and important, written at the peak of his powers and the height of his career.

In Shakespeare's time, plays got audiences very excited. Some politicians thought this might be useful. A man named Sir Gilly Meyrick asked the Lord Chamberlain's Men to perform *Richard II* on February 7, 1601. In Shakespeare's play, King Richard breaks his own laws and is overthrown by his cousin. In England at that time, some men were planning to do just that to Queen Elizabeth. Meyrick thought the play would inspire them to revolt. Shakespeare's troupe did perform the play, and the earl of Essex, the leader of the group, did try to overthrow the queen, but failed. Shakespeare and his players were in big trouble, but they talked their way out of it and only had to perform a play for the queen as their punishment—on the night before the earl's execution.

In February 1603, the queen died at age 69. Her cousin James became King James I. The new king liked Shakespeare's plays as much as Queen Elizabeth had, and he gave money to the company. He offered the company a royal license, which allowed them to call themselves the King's Men. With their name change, they were given cloth to make special uniforms called livery. The company also regularly entertained the king at court.

Like Queen Elizabeth I, King James I of England was a patron of the arts.

The patronage of the king of England had made Shakespeare and his acting com-pany very successful. They dressed in the king's colors, they performed in the king's court, and they bore the name of the king. The King's Men was London's leading theatrical group. Shakespeare created some of his most important work during this time.

In 1608, Shakespeare's company added an indoor

theater, Blackfriars, with a full roof that allowed them to perform plays in winter as well as summer. It had artificial lighting and was probably heated as well. This year also marks the beginning of the fourth and final period of Shakespeare's career. During this period, he wrote four plays. These final plays are *Cymbeline, The Winter's Tale, The Tempest*, and *Henry VIII*. Scholars believe that he may have written the history play *Henry VIII* with another playwright, John Fletcher.

Most Shakespeare experts agree that only a small percentage of his work was autobiographical. Shakespeare wrote more about the many people he came in contact with in life than he did about himself. Yet many Shakespeare biographers suggest that *The Tempest*, one of his final works, reflected many of the issues he was no doubt facing in his own life.

In *The Tempest*, the main character, Prospero, has many magical powers that he uses throughout the play to correct a series of wrongs and set people on the proper course for their lives. At the end of the play, when all has been made right with the world, Prospero gives up his magical abilities and states, "Let your indulgence set me free." Many scholars believe that Shakespeare used the character of Prospero to announce that his writing powers were leaving him, or that he was ready to put down his pen.

Shakespeare was not yet finished writing, however. He wrote several more plays, but he seemed to be winding down and preparing to start a new chapter in his life.

Shakespeare's plays had already changed the face of English theater forever. His writing transformed plays from simple, clumsy comedies and boring histories into funny, wise, and very human theater. It was a great deal to have accomplished in one lifetime. Perhaps Shakespeare was ready to retire. Perhaps he just wanted a change from London. In any case, around 1611, Shakespeare went home to Stratford.

William was 47, Anne was 54, and his daughters were in their mid-20's. Shakespeare moved into New Place with Anne and enjoyed small town life again. He kept his own half-pint mug down at the local

New Place, once located at this site, was the second-largest home in Stratford.

tavern where he drank every Saturday afternoon. His daughter Susanna and her husband lived nearby, and he saw them often. He didn't write plays for Stratford since there was no acting company or theater in town. Besides, the town banned plays as being evil.

Though he no longer lived in London, Shakespeare still owned part of the theater company. On June 29, 1613, disaster struck. During a performance of *Henry VIII* at the Globe Theatre, a special effects cannon accidentally sparked a fire on the straw half roof. Within an hour, the entire theater burned to the ground. No one was hurt, though one man's pants caught fire and were extinguished with a bottle of ale. A new Globe was rebuilt on the site within the year. This time, it was built with a tiled roof.

Shakespeare's new Globe Theatre continued operating as a theater until 1642, when it was closed down by the Puritans. In 1644, the theater was demolished in order to build apartments on the site. In 1993, construction began on a new Globe Theatre near the site of the original. It was officially opened by Queen Elizabeth II in May 1997 with a production of Henry V. This new Globe is reproduced according to scholars' knowledge of the original Globe.

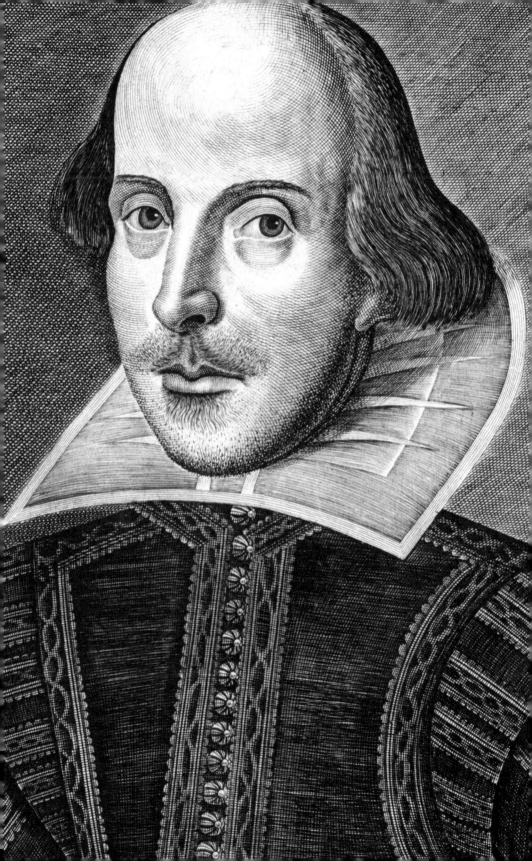

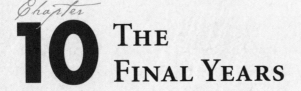

10 THE FINAL YEARS

Chapter

ᶜᵛᵛᵛᵛᵛᵒ

On February 10, 1616, Shakespeare's daughter Judith married Thomas Quiney, a wine merchant who was the son of a neighbor in Stratford. At the wedding reception, Shakespeare is said to have drunk too much with old friends, including fellow writer Ben Jonson, and caught a fever that eventually killed him. But many Shakespeare scholars do not believe this story and believe instead that he became ill as he aged.

Just six weeks after Judith's wedding, Shakespeare revised his will. His signature looks a bit shaky, as though he were weak or sick. In his will, Shakespeare left specific household items and homes to his children. He wrote that his wife should receive his "second-best bed." Was this an insult to

An engraving of Shakespeare was printed on the title page of the 1623 First Folio, the first printed collection of Shakespeare's plays.

Anne Hathaway? Perhaps. Some historians say that the second-best bed in a large house was the bed the man and wife slept in, and they saved the best bed for guests. If that is true, then this does not seem like an insult. Other Shakespeare scholars say that the best bed was the one Shakespeare was occupying in his illness, and he did not want to leave her his sickbed. We will never know for sure.

Shakespeare's signature on his 1616 will is shaky, suggesting that his health might have been poor.

Shakespeare's most valuable possessions—his poems and plays—were not mentioned. He could not have imagined how many people would be reading his plays and memorizing his poetry over the coming centuries.

William Shakespeare died at home on April 23, 1616, at age 52. He was buried in Holy Trinity Church in Stratford. His gravestone bears a curse in the-odd-looking spelling common in his time: "Good Frend for Jesus sake forbeare, To digg the dust enclosed heare: Bleste be ye man that spares these stones, and curst be he that moves my bones." A stonemason named Gheerart Janssen, who worked near the Globe Theatre, carved a bust of Shakespeare. It was painted and placed on Shakespeare's tomb in the church.

In Shakespeare's time, cemetery space was at a premium, and sometimes old graves were dug up so that new graves could be put in their place. Shakespeare's curse must have worked; his grave has remained undisturbed since his death.

Anne lived on for seven years after her husband died. Their daughter Susanna had married a doctor named John Hall in 1607 and gave birth to a daughter, Elizabeth, in 1608. Although Elizabeth married twice, she died childless at 61 years old.

Shakespeare's daughter Judith, who had married in 1616, had three sons, one named Shakespeare Quiney, who died as a baby. Their other two sons died when they were young men. Judith died at the age of 77.

Although William Shakespeare had no male descendants to carry on the family name, the fame

GOOD FREND FOR IESVS SAKE FORBEARE,
TO DICG THE DVST ENCLOASED HEARE.
BLESE BE Y MAN Y SPARES THES STONES
AND CVRST BE HE Y MOVES MY BONES.

Shakespeare's gravestone bears a warning that has been heeded for more than 400 years.

he achieved after his death has made the Shakespeare name live on.

William Shakespeare grew up as a young boy with an ordinary education, married young, and left his family behind to go to London and make his fortune as a writer of plays, an actor, and a part-owner in an acting company. When he was a teenager, the first professional theater companies in London opened. By the time he turned 30 years old, he was a member of one of the first two important theater companies in London. When he died 20 years later, he had his own theater company and was a well-to-do landowner in his hometown of Stratford.

If an author today had as many books in print and sold as many books as Shakespeare, he or she would be very rich. Yet Shakespeare did not try to get his plays printed. In his day, bookstores did not exist. Books were made by hand. Only the rich owned books, and only the well-educated could read them. Still, writers did have poems and stories published, and people did buy books. Fortunately, his friends and the actors in his theater saved Shakespeare's plays and published them after he died.

When Shakespeare died in 1616, his acting company, the King's Men, was famous and wealthy. Much of this they owed to Shakespeare. As a memorial to their friend and fellow actor, members of his company decided to gather together his works and publish them. They no doubt knew that publishing the popular plays would earn them money. Two members, John Heminges and Henry Condell, went through the actors' scripts and pieced together versions of the plays. It took them about seven years.

On November 8, 1623, their work, entitled *Mr. William*

Today, there are still repertory companies that perform only Shakespeare's work. Some even perform it outside, as Shakespeare's own troupes did, in performances called "Shakespeare in the Park."

Shakespeare's Comedies, Histories, and Tragedies, was published. This publication was called the First Folio of 1623. A folio was not quite a book. Like the earlier quartos, a folio was folded paper, and buyers had to find their own covers. Ben Jonson, another important writer and playwright of the time, wrote a moving introduction to the folio. The First Folio included 36 plays and cost one pound in British money. About 250 copies of the First Folio still exist, and each is worth more than $2 million.

The 1623 first printing of the First Folio sold out, and a second printing was made about nine years

Shakespeare's friend Ben Jonson wrote the introduction to the 1623 First Folio.

To the Reader.

This Figure, that thou here feeſt put,
    It was for gentle Shakeſpeare cut;
Wherein the Grauer had a ſtrife
    with Nature, to out-doo the life :
O, could he but haue drawne his wit
    As well in braſſe, as he hath hit
His face ; the Print would then ſurpaſſe
    All, that vvas euer vvrit in braſſe.
But, ſince he cannot, Reader, looke
    Not on his Picture, but his Booke.

                    B. I.

later. Two more versions were printed before 1700, with sonnets and other work of Shakespeare's added to the contents. The printed plays made it easier for other acting companies across England and Europe to perform Shakespeare, and his name and fame spread. More versions of his plays were being printed, and more people read Shakespeare and quoted his lines. As the centuries passed, Shakespeare's works were added to literature textbooks all over the world. Most students read Shakespeare poems or plays sometime during their schooling.

Over the years, some people have doubted that one man could write so many masterpieces or that a country boy could grow up to write so knowledgeably about kings and royalty. Some scholars have found the contrast between Shakespeare's education and the genius of his writing to be so great that they have suggested that Shakespeare couldn't possibly have written all of his works by himself. Some question whether he wrote any of them at all. How could this common man from a small village with only a basic education possibly write some of the greatest works in history?

The way printers worked at that time, publishing writing without the author's permission or slapping any author's name on anything they pleased, only confuses the issue. Shakespeare was a common name at the time, and some scholars wonder if an educated nobleman or even other writers of the time such as Ben Jonson or Christopher Marlowe might have used "Shakespeare" as a false name for some of their work. Or perhaps they collaborated with Shakespeare on certain plays, contributing ideas or taking turns writing parts. This sort of collaboration was common in Shakespeare's time.

Scholars have also suggested a number of other possible authors for the works, including the queen of England from Shakespeare's time, Elizabeth I herself. Others suggest that the author may have been Francis Bacon, a great scholar of the Elizabethan era.

But it seems unlikely that while Shakespeare's plays were becoming famous—or even after Shakespeare's own death—no "true" author stepped forward to claim credit. And today, few Shakespeare scholars doubt that anyone but Shakespeare himself is responsible for the incredible body of work.

Look up any list of the greatest books ever written, and the complete works of William Shakespeare will certainly be listed there. His plays have been filmed as movies and choreographed for the ballet. And with the thousands of new words and expressions he invented, Shakespeare forever changed the English language.

Even today, when generations of new writers

Romeo and Juliet meet at a masked ball in a ballet version of Shakespeare's famous play.

have produced entire bookstores of bestsellers, William Shakespeare, who lived 400 years ago, is considered by many to be the best and most important writer the world has known.

As his friend Ben Jonson said, "He was not of an age, but for all time!" ✍

SHAKESPEARE'S LIFE

1564

Born on or around
April 23; baptized
on April 26 at Holy
Trinity Church in
Stratford, England

1570

1558

Elizabeth I is
crowned in England,
beginning a 45-year
reign as queen

1570

The potato is
introduced to Europe
from South America

WORLD EVENTS

1582

Marries Anne
Hathaway

1585

Twins Judith and
Hamnet born

1583

First daughter,
Susanna, born in May

1585

English explorer Sir
Francis Drake
embarks on a journey
to capture Spanish
treasure ships in the
West Indies

1580

William Bourne
makes the first
published description
of a submarine

SHAKESPEARE'S LIFE

BETWEEN 1585 AND 1592

Leaves Stratford and joins a traveling acting company

1593

Publishes first narrative poem, *Venus and Adonis*

1585

1588

The English navy and merchant ships defeat the Spanish armada off the coast of France

1592

Japan launches an unsuccessful invasion of Korea

WORLD EVENTS

1596

Applies for and
receives a coat of
arms; son Hamnet dies

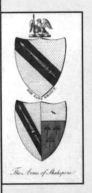

1594

Publishes narrative
poem, *The Rape of
Lucrece*

1599

Builds Globe Theatre
in a London suburb

1595

1597

The great English
scientist Francis Bacon
publishes Essays

1595

English royal forces
and Irish chieftains
battle for control of
Northern Ireland

SHAKESPEARE'S LIFE

1609

Sonnets are published

SHAKE-SPEARES

S O N N E T S.

Neuer before Imprinted.

AT LONDON
By *G. Eld* for *T. T.* and are
to be folde by *John Wright,* dwelling
at Chrift Church gate.
1 6 0 9.

1608

Blackfriars Theatre
built

1600

1607

Jamestown, Virginia,
the first English set-
tlement on the North
American mainland,
is founded

1608

Galileo constructs
the first astronomical
telescope

WORLD EVENTS

1611

Returns to Stratford
to live with his family
after more than 20
years in London

1613

The Globe Theatre
burns and is rebuilt

1616

Dies on April 23

1615

1611

The King James Bible,
commissioned by
the British king,
is published

1614

Pocahontas marries
John Rolfe

DATE OF BIRTH: Unknown; probably April 23, 1564

BIRTHPLACE: Stratford, England

FATHER: John Shakespeare

MOTHER: Mary Arden Shakespeare

EDUCATION: Grammar school

SPOUSE: Anne Hathaway (1556–1623)

DATE OF MARRIAGE: 1582

CHILDREN: Susanna (1583–1649)
Judith (1585–1662)
Hamnet (1585–1596)

DATE OF DEATH: April 23, 1616

PLACE OF BURIAL: Holy Trinity Church, Stratford, England

In the Library

Aagesen, Colleen. *Shakespeare for Kids: His Life and Times.* Chicago: Chicago Review Press, 1999.

Aliki. *William Shakespeare & the Globe.* New York: HarperTrophy, 2000.

Burdett, Lois. *Romeo and Juliet: For Kids.* Willowdale, Ontario: Firefly Books, 1998.

Krull, Kathleen. *Lives of the Writers: Comedies, Tragedies (and What the Neighbors Thought).* New York: Harcourt Brace & Company, 1994.

Miller, Carol Rawlings. *Irresistible Shakespeare.* New York: Scholastic Professional Books, 2001.

Nesbit, E. *The Children's Shakespeare.* Chicago: Academy Chicago Publishers, 2000

Stanley, Diane. *Bard of Avon: The Story of William Shakespeare.* New York: HarperTrophy, 1998.

Look for more Signature Lives
books about this era:

Christopher Columbus: *Explorer of the New World*
ISBN 0-7565-0811-8

Nicolaus Copernicus: *Father of Modern Astronomy*
ISBN 0-7565-1812-6

Elizabeth I: *Queen of Tudor England*
ISBN 0-7565-0988-2

Galileo: *Astronomer and Physicist*
ISBN 0-7565-0813-4

Johannes Gutenberg: *Inventor of the Printing Press*
ISBN 0-7565-0989-0

Michelangelo: *Sculptor and Painter*
ISBN 0-7565-0814-2

Francisco Pizarro: *Conqueror of the Incas*
ISBN 0-7565-0815-0

ON THE WEB

For more information on *William Shakespeare*, use FactHound to track down Web sites related to this book.

1. Go to *www.facthound.com*
2. Type in a search word related to this book or this book ID: 0756508169
3. Click on the *Fetch It* button.

FactHound will find the best Web sites for you

HISTORIC SITES

Folger Shakespeare Library
201 E. Capitol St. S.E.
Washington, DC 20003
201/544-7077
To see the world's largest collection of Shakespeare's works, statues of famous charactes, and other exhibits

The Heart of America Shakespeare Festival
Southmoreland Park
47th and Oak Streets
Kansas City, MO 64112
816/531-7728
To see Shakespeare's plays performed at an annual festival celebrating his work

apprenticed
bound to a skilled person in order to learn a trade or a craft

ballads
songs that tell stories

catechism
religious instruction that is often conducted in the form of questions and answers

christened
accepted into the Christian religion in a special ceremony

gentry
the upper or ruling class, especially those who are entitled to bear a coat of arms

livery
a uniform worn by members of a profession

master craftsman
a worker who practices a trade with special skill

patron
someone who gives money to a person in order to support his or her work

playbill
an advertisement for a play

playwright
someone who writes plays

props
an item that an actor carries or uses in a theater production

repertor
a company that presents several different plays in the course of a season at one theater

revolt
to fight against an authority

scholar
a person who studies and researches a subject, often at a college or university

sonnet
a poem with 14 lines and a fixed pattern of rhymes

stonemason
one who builds or works with stone

troupe
a group of theatrical performers

will
a legal document leaving instructions for who receives what property after the owner's death

Chapter 3

Page 11, line 7: William Shakespeare. *As You Like It.* Act II, scene 7.

Chapter 4

Page 32, line 16: William Shakespeare. *Hamlet.* Act I, scene 3.

Chapter 6

Page 49, line 23: Anthony Holden. *William Shakespeare: The Man Behind the Genius.* London: Little, Brown, 1999, p. 231.

Chapter 8

Page 74, line 27: William Shakespeare. *Henry V.* Prologue.

Page 76, line 11: William Shakespeare. *As You Like It.* Act II, scene 7.

Page 76, line 18: William Shakespeare. *The Merchant of Venice.* Act I, scene 1.

Chapter 9

Page 83, line 17: William Shakespeare. *The Tempest.* Epilogue.

Chapter 10

Page 87. line 15: Joyce Rogers. *The Second Best Bed: Shakespeare's Will in a New Light.* Westport, Conn.: Greenwood Press, 1993, pp. 74–75.

Page 95, line 6: Ben Jonson. *Preface to 1623 First Folio.* http://shakespeare.palomar.edu/Folio1.htm#Beloved

Duncan-Jones, Katherine. *Ungentle Shakespeare: Scenes From His Life.* London: The Arden Shakespeare, 2001.

Fraser, Russell. *Shakespeare: The Later Years.* New York: Columbia University Press, 1992.

Gurr, Andrew. *William Shakespeare: The Extraordinary Life of the Most Successful Writer of All Time.* New York: HarperCollins, 1995.

Holden, Anthony. *William Shakespeare: The Man Behind the Genius.* London: Little, Brown, 1999.

Krull, Kathleen. *Lives of the Writers: Comedies, Tragedies (and What the Neighbors Thought).* New York: Harcourt Brace & Company, 1994.

Price, Diana. *Shakespeare's Unorthodox Biography: New Evidence of an Authorship Problem.* Westport, Conn.: Greenwood Press, 2001.

Rogers, Joyce. *The Second Best Bed: Shakespeare's Will in a New Light.* Westport, Conn.: Greenwood Press, 1993.

Sams, Eric. *The Real Shakespeare: Retrieving the Early Years, 1564-1594.* New Haven, Conn.: Yale University Press, 1999.

Pamela Hill Nettleton is the author of several nonfiction books for children. She writes essays and features for magazines and is the author of *Getting Married When It's Not Your First Time*.

Image Credits